Hare's Big Tug-of-War

An African Fable

retold by Cheyenne Cisco

illustrated by Mary Watson

HARCOURT BRACE & COMPANY

Orlando Atlanta Austin Boston San Francisco Chicago Dallas New York
Toronto London

2

One morning, Hare woke up and looked out his window. Big Elephant sat on one side of the garden, eating Hare's carrots!

Big Hippo sat on the other side of the garden, eating Hare's beets! "Those are mine!" Hare shouted. "Leave them alone!" But Big Elephant and Big Hippo ate and ate.

5

6

The next day, Hare got a rope and saw Big Elephant. "Let's have a tug-of-war," he said to Big Elephant.

"HA HA HA!" shouted Big Elephant. "You can't beat me!" He took one end of the rope.

Then Hare took a boat across the river and saw Big Hippo. "Let's have a tug-of-war," he said to Big Hippo.

"HO HO HO!" shouted Big Hippo. "You can't beat me!" He took the other end of the rope.

9

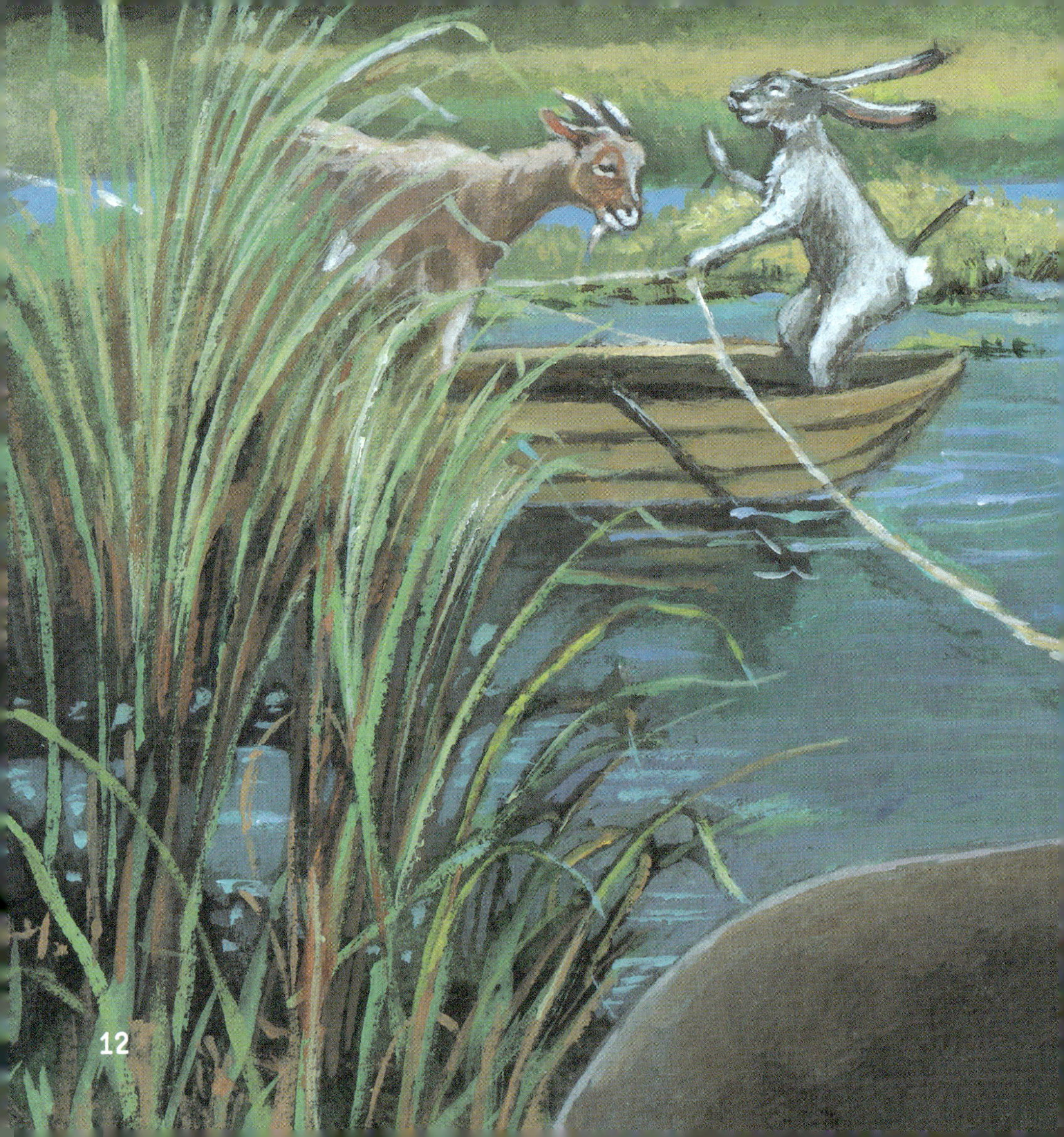

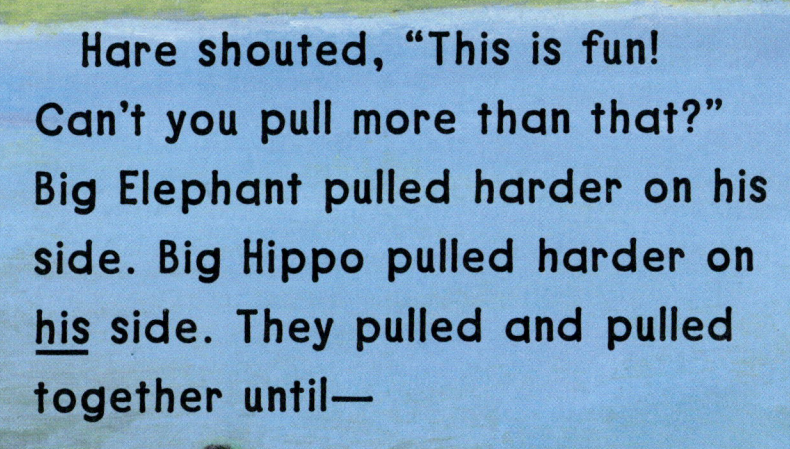

Hare shouted, "This is fun! Can't you pull more than that?" Big Elephant pulled harder on his side. Big Hippo pulled harder on <u>his</u> side. They pulled and pulled together until—

Hare's goat cut the rope in the middle.

15

And that is how Hare won the big tug-of-war.